The Full Life
Gratitude
Journal
for M♥ms

A daily gratitude journal for a full life
that is more grateful, mindful, and joyful

The Full Life Gratitude Journal for Moms by Autumn McKay
Published by Creative Ideas Publishing

www.bestmomideas.com

For permissions contact:
permissions@bestmomideas.com

Graphic design by Sheila Durden

ISBN: 978-1-952016-00-4

Introduction

We all want a happy life, a fantastic job, a perfect family, and financial freedom. While in pursuit of this "perfect" life, how often do we take a minute to be thankful for what we already have or have already accomplished?

Gratitude is a feeling of being thankful. This feeling is usually something we focus on during the holiday season. Instead of being grateful just once a year, what if we decided to make it a daily habit. How would our lives change?

Gratitude is a powerful emotion. Many studies have found there are benefits of practicing gratitude. Here are a few:

- ✓ Gratitude makes you happier. Journaling for five minutes a day about what we are grateful for can increase our long-term happiness by over 10%. When we notice what we already have we feel more positive about our lives.

- ✓ Gratitude increases our self-esteem. Gratitude can help you feel better about your circumstances, which can lead to feeling better about yourself.

- ✓ Gratitude can make you more patient. Research shows that people who felt grateful for the little, everyday things were more patient compared to those who didn't find gratitude on a daily basis.

- ✓ Gratitude can improve your relationships. Feeling grateful toward your spouse, children, or loved ones can improve the feeling of connection between each other.

- ✓ Gratitude can help in times of stress. When you are able to find the positive in your life you are more equipped to deal with difficult situations.

- ✓ Gratitude makes us more optimistic. Expressing our gratitude helps us to feel and think more positively. Gratitude journaling has been shown to increase our optimism between 5-15%. The more we think about what we are grateful for, the more we find things to be grateful for.

- ✓ Gratitude makes us less materialistic. Those who are more grateful tend to be less materialistic because we appreciate what we already have and do not find it necessary to obtain more things in order to be happy. We are more satisfied.

✓ Gratitude makes us more effective parents, employers, or employees. Practicing gratitude enhances your praise-giving and motivating abilities so you are better equipped to motivate those around you.

✓ Gratitude helps us be better decision makers. When we are grateful we are better able to see long-term goals and make decisions that lead us to those goals rather than seeking short-term gratification.

✓ Gratitude improves your overall physical health. Evidence shows that the more grateful a person is the more likely they are to take care of themselves through exercise, eating better and even improved sleep.

Practicing gratitude is simple words of love and praise or thankfulness that helps us acknowledge the blessings in our lives. It helps us control how we feel about each thing or situation in our lives. Robin Sharma put it beautifully:

"Gratitude drives happiness. Happiness boosts productivity. Productivity reveals mastery. And mastery inspires the world."

My Story

I'm a wife to a wonderful husband. I have three happy, healthy children who I love. I'm also an author, caregiver to my family, full-time chef, healer of boo-boos, cheerleader, maid, planner of playground visits, and finder of lost toys. I love my life, but to be honest, I started to get burned out with all these responsibilities.

I found myself not being the best mom or wife I could be or had been. I was losing my patience too easily with my children. I just seemed to wake up on the wrong side of the bed more often than I should have—in fact, every side of my bed must have been the wrong side of the bed, or at least that's how it felt.

At the time, my husband had been discovering the practice of gratitude through meditation. I saw a transformation in his attitude and an amplified appreciation for me and our children. I was encouraged by his change, and decided I would try mediation as well. I tried it for a week. I would wake up, sit in a quiet space for ten minutes and focus on three things I was grateful for during that time. I began to notice how my attitude started to shift as I was mentally looking for things to be thankful for in my next meditation time.

However, I often found my mind wandering during meditation, so I decided to start journaling for my meditation time instead. I tried several journaling techniques, but found my perfect recipe of things to focus on for a great day. During my journal time I write down three gratitudes, my goal for the day, and have a time of prayer and reflection. I also use this time to reflect on my long term goals to help give me prospective of what I want for myself and my family.

Practicing gratitude through journaling has helped me to improve my patience with the ones I love, be more optimistic, respond to my children instead of react, appreciate the people and things in my life, and lower my stress level. I also give practicing gratitude credit for making me much more mentally strong which helped me survive two miscarriages in 2019.

In short, I've become really passionate about this simple daily practice because it has so drastically changed my life in only a few months. My hope as you begin your gratitude journey is that you are able to find joy as you live a life you love each and every day!

I would love to hear your gratitude story, so please email me at autumn@ bestmomideas.com to share your journey!

How to Use

In order to reap the benefits of practicing gratitude, I recommend using this journal on a daily basis. However, you can use it at any time of day you choose. I like to start my day by journaling, but you might find that it's better for you to journal before bed, at lunch, before you begin work, or while you are eating breakfast. Whenever you choose to journal, it helps to practice gratitude at the same time everyday so that it starts to become part of your daily routine. I also find it helpful to find a quiet space free from distractions.

At the top of each journaling page you will find an inspiring quote, an uplifting Bible verse, or a challenge to help you grow. I encourage you to read or take part in these challenges to help motivate you and continue on this journey.

Then you can list three things you are grateful for. You may choose to focus on something in the past, like a childhood memory or a lesson you learned. You may choose to be grateful for something in the present, like this new day you have been given or this quiet time to yourself. Or you may choose to be grateful for what's to come, like an upcoming vacation. Whatever you choose to be thankful for, write it down, and take a minute to breathe and focus on those gratitudes.

I find it helpful to write down a goal for the day—this is one thing I want to make sure I accomplish for the day. This helps me to make sure I keep my day focused so I don't get distracted by the little things that pop up throughout the day. Sometimes my goal is to complete a project for work, clean the kitchen, plan meals for the following week, or even rest. I encourage you to write down a daily goal.

I like to write down a long-term goal to help remind me what I want for myself and my family's future. This long-term goal is often the same goal each day until it is accomplished, but it helps drives me. Having the long-term goal written down each day helps me to make sure my daily goals are driving me to meet my long-term goal. So, I encourage you to think about a long-term goal you want for yourself or your family. This can be financial freedom, go on a vacation, lose weight, workout regularly, buy a house or anything—the possibilities are endless.

Daily affirmations are another way to focus on things you are grateful for about yourself. Often times we tend to focus on things we don't like about ourselves, so instead choose to focus on things you or other people love about yourself. These can be physical, mental, or personality attributes that make you special.

The space for prayer or reflection is optional to use. After I have had time to focus on my gratitudes I like to thank my Creator for providing me with these things or giving me the abilities to accomplish my goals. I also use it as a time to talk to God and ask for His guidance, healing, or wisdom.

Later in the evening or during the following journal time you can think about a win you had from your day. A win is something that made the day great! It can be that you accomplished your goal, you practiced gratitude, you didn't drink a sugary drink, or anything that made your day great. Write it down.

My children made up the word "sooga." It means a feeling greater than awesome. I want your days to be sooga, so think of something that could have made your day even better or a lesson you learned and write it down. You don't have to dwell on it. Writing it down helps you to remember what you learned and hopefully change your actions for the better the next time you are faced with a similar situation.

I hope you begin to see a transformation in the way you view yourself and the world around you as you practice gratitude daily!

Date: _____ / _____ / _____

I will praise the name of God with a song; I will magnify him with thanksgiving.
Psalm 69:30 (ESV)

Today, I am grateful for...

1. ....
2. ....
3. ....

Goal for today...

....

Long-term goal I want to remember....

....

Daily affirmations—I am...

1. ....
2. ....

Time for prayer or reflection...

....
....
....
....
....

One win I had today was...

....
....

How could I have made today even better?

....
....

Date: .... / .... / ....

"Enjoy the little things, for one day you may look back and realize they were the big things."
–Robert Brault

Today, I am grateful for...

1. ....
2. ....
3. ....

Goal for today...

....

Long-term goal I want to remember....

....

Daily affirmations—I am...

1. ....
2. ....

Time for prayer or reflection...

....
....
....
....
....

One win I had today was...

....
....

How could I have made today even better?

....
....

Date: .... / .... / ....

"As we express our gratitude, we must never forget that the highest appreciation is not to utter words but to live by them." –John F. Kennedy

Today, I am grateful for...

1. ....
2. ....
3. ....

Goal for today...

....

Long-term goal I want to remember....

....

Daily affirmations—I am...

1. ....
2. ....

Time for prayer or reflection...

....
....
....
....

One win I had today was...

....
....

How could I have made today even better?

....
....

Date: .... / .... / ....

"Reflect upon your present blessing, of which every man has plenty;
not on your past misfortunes, of which all men have some." –Charles Dickens

Today, I am grateful for...

1. ....
2. ....
3. ....

Goal for today...

....

Long-term goal I want to remembner....

....

Daily affirmations—I am...

1. ....
2. ....

Time for prayer or reflection...

....
....
....
....
....

One win I had today was...

....
....

How could I have made today even better?

....
....

Date: .... / .... / ....

 Let us come into his presence with thanksgiving; let us make a joyful noise to him with songs of praise! Psalm 95:2 (ESV)

Today, I am grateful for...

1. ....
2. ....
3. ....

Goal for today...

....

Long-term goal I want to remember....

....

Daily affirmations—I am...

1. ....
2. ....

Time for prayer or reflection...

....
....
....
....
....

One win I had today was...

....
....

How could I have made today even better?

....
....

Date: .... / .... / ....

 "In essence, if we want to direct our lives, we must take control of our consistent actions. It's not what we do once in a while that shapes our lives, but what we do consistently." –Tony Robbins

Today, I am grateful for...

1. ....
2. ....
3. ....

Goal for today...

....

Long-term goal I want to remember....

....

Daily affirmations—I am...

1. ....
2. ....

Time for prayer or reflection...

....
....
....
....

One win I had today was...

....
....

How could I have made today even better?

....
....

Date:

 Challenge: *Seek someone out, and offer them a compliment.*

Today, I am grateful for...

1. ....
2. ....
3. ....

Goal for today...

....

Long-term goal I want to remember....

....

Daily affirmations—I am...

1. ....
2. ....

Time for prayer or reflection...

....
....
....
....
....

One win I had today was...

....
....

How could I have made today even better?

....
....

Date: .... / .... / ....

*"Everyone has inside them a piece of good news. The good news is you don't know
how great you can be! How much you can love! What you can accomplish!
And what your potential is." – Anne Frank*

Today, I am grateful for...

1. ....
2. ....
3. ....

Goal for today...

....

Long-term goal I want to remember....

....

Daily affirmations—I am...

1. ....
2. ....

Time for prayer or reflection...

....
....
....
....
....

One win I had today was...

....
....

How could I have made today even better?

....
....

Date: _____ / _____ / _____

"Continuous effort - not strength or intelligence - is the key to unlocking our potential."
—*Winston S. Churchill*

Today, I am grateful for...

1. ....
2. ....
3. ....

Goal for today...

....

Long-term goal I want to remember....

....

Daily affirmations—I am...

1. ....
2. ....

Time for prayer or reflection...

....
....
....
....
....

One win I had today was...

....
....

How could I have made today even better?

....
....

Date: .... / .... / ....

 Enter his gates with thanksgiving, and his courts with praise! Give thanks to him; bless his name!
Psalm 100:4 (ESV)

Today, I am grateful for...

1. ....
2. ....
3. ....

Goal for today...

....

Long-term goal I want to remember....

....

Daily affirmations—I am...

1. ....
2. ....

Time for prayer or reflection...

....
....
....
....
....

One win I had today was...

....
....

How could I have made today even better?

....
....

Date: .... / .... / ....

 "Acknowledging the good that you already have in your life is the foundation for all abundance."
–Eckhart Tolle

Today, I am grateful for...

1. ....
2. ....
3. ....

Goal for today...

....

Long-term goal I want to remember....

....

Daily affirmations—I am...

1. ....
2. ....

Time for prayer or reflection...

....
....
....
....

One win I had today was...

....
....

How could I have made today even better?

....
....

Date: .... / .... / ....

*"The world has enough beautiful mountains and meadows, spectacular skies and serene lakes.
It has enough lush forests, flowered fields, and sandy beaches. It has plenty of stars and
the promise of a new sunrise and sunset every day. What the world needs more of
is people to appreciate and enjoy it." —Michael Josephson*

Today, I am grateful for...

1. ....
2. ....
3. ....

Goal for today...

....

Long-term goal I want to remember....

....

Daily affirmations—I am...

1. ....
2. ....

Time for prayer or reflection...

....
....
....
....

One win I had today was...

....
....

How could I have made today even better?

....

Date: _____ / _____ / _____

"It is time for us all to stand and cheer for the doer, the achiever – the one who recognizes the challenges and does something about it." —Vince Lombardi

Today, I am grateful for...

1. ....
2. ....
3. ....

Goal for today...

....

Long-term goal I want to remember....

....

Daily affirmations—I am...

1. ....
2. ....

Time for prayer or reflection...

....
....
....
....
....

One win I had today was...

....
....

How could I have made today even better?

....
....

Date: _____ / _____ / _____

Challenge: *Donate one item that no longer sparks joy.*

Today, I am grateful for...

1. ....
2. ....
3. ....

Goal for today...

....

Long-term goal I want to remember....

....

Daily affirmations—I am...

1. ....
2. ....

Time for prayer or reflection...

....
....
....
....
....

One win I had today was...

....
....

How could I have made today even better?

....
....

Date: ..../.........../.............

*Let them thank the Lord for his steadfast love, for his wondrous works to the children of man!
And let them offer sacrifices of thanksgiving, and tell of his deeds
in songs of joy! Psalm 107:21-22 (ESV)*

Today, I am grateful for...

1. ....
2. ....
3. ....

Goal for today...

....

Long-term goal I want to remember....

....

Daily affirmations—I am...

1. ....
2. ....

Time for prayer or reflection...

....
....
....
....
....

One win I had today was...

....
....

How could I have made today even better?

....
....

Date: _____ / _____ / _____

 "Be thankful for what you have; you'll end up having more. If you concentrate on what you don't have, you will never, ever have enough." —Oprah Winfrey

Today, I am grateful for...

1. ....
2. ....
3. ....

Goal for today...

....

Long-term goal I want to remember....

....

Daily affirmations—I am...

1. ....
2. ....

Time for prayer or reflection...

....
....
....
....

One win I had today was...

....
....

How could I have made today even better?

....
....

Date: _____ / _____ / _____

"Fall seven times, stand up eight."
—Japanese Proverb

Today, I am grateful for...

1. ....
2. ....
3. ....

Goal for today...

....

Long-term goal I want to remember....

....

Daily affirmations—I am...

1. ....
2. ....

Time for prayer or reflection...

....
....
....
....
....

One win I had today was...

....
....

How could I have made today even better?

....
....

Date: .... / .... / ....

"When I started counting my blessings, my whole life turned around."
—Willie Nelson

Today, I am grateful for...

1. ....
2. ....
3. ....

Goal for today...

....

Long-term goal I want to remember....

....

Daily affirmations—I am...

1. ....
2. ....

Time for prayer or reflection...

....
....
....
....
....

One win I had today was...

....
....

How could I have made today even better?

....
....

Date: .... / .... / ....

"If you woke up this morning, you have reason to be grateful. If you lie your head on a pillow tonight, you have reason to give thanks. Don't take a single day for grated. They run out." —Toni Sorenson

Today, I am grateful for...

1. ....
2. ....
3. ....

Goal for today...

....

Long-term goal I want to remember....

....

Daily affirmations—I am...

1. ....
2. ....

Time for prayer or reflection...

....
....
....
....

One win I had today was...

....
....

How could I have made today even better?

....
....

Date: _____ / _____ / _____

"Gratitude and attitude are not challenges; they are choices."
—Robert Braathe

Today, I am grateful for...

1. ....
2. ....
3. ....

Goal for today...

....

Long-term goal I want to remember....

....

Daily affirmations—I am...

1. ....
2. ....

Time for prayer or reflection...

....
....
....
....
....

One win I had today was...

....
....

How could I have made today even better?

....
....

Date: _____ / _____ / _____

"In life, one has a choice to take one of two paths: to wait for some special day--or to celebrate each special day." —Rasheed Ogunlaru

Today, I am grateful for...

1. ....
2. ....
3. ....

Goal for today...

....

Long-term goal I want to remember....

....

Daily affirmations—I am...

1. ....
2. ....

Time for prayer or reflection...

....
....
....
....
....

One win I had today was...

....
....

How could I have made today even better?

....
....

Date: _____ / _____ / _____

Challenge: *Tell someone you love them.*

Today, I am grateful for...

1. ....
2. ....
3. ....

Goal for today...

....

Long-term goal I want to remember....

....

Daily affirmations—I am...

1. ....
2. ....

Time for prayer or reflection...

....
....
....
....

One win I had today was...

....
....

How could I have made today even better?

....
....

Date: ...... / ...... / ......

Today, I am grateful for...

1. ....
2. ....
3. ....

Goal for today...

....

Long-term goal I want to remember....

....

Daily affirmations—I am...

1. ....
2. ....

Time for prayer or reflection...

....
....
....
....
....

One win I had today was...

....
....

How could I have made today even better?

....
....

Date: .... / .... / ....

Gracious is the Lord, and righteous; our God is merciful.
Psalm 116:5 (ESV)

Today, I am grateful for...

1. ....
2. ....
3. ....

Goal for today...

....

Long-term goal I want to remember....

....

Daily affirmations—I am...

1. ....
2. ....

Time for prayer or reflection...

....
....
....
....
....

One win I had today was...

....
....

How could I have made today even better?

....
....

Date: .... / .... / ....

 "It is only with gratitude that life becomes rich."
—Dietrich Bonhoeffer

Today, I am grateful for...

1. ....
2. ....
3. ....

Goal for today...

....

Long-term goal I want to remember....

....

Daily affirmations—I am...

1. ....
2. ....

Time for prayer or reflection...

....
....
....
....
....

One win I had today was...

....
....

How could I have made today even better?

....
....

Date: .... / .... / ....

"It is not joy that makes us grateful; it is gratitude that makes us joyful."
—David Steindl-Rast

Today, I am grateful for...

1. ....
2. ....
3. ....

Goal for today...

....

Long-term goal I want to remember....

....

Daily affirmations—I am...

1. ....
2. ....

Time for prayer or reflection...

....
....
....
....
....

One win I had today was...

....
....

How could I have made today even better?

....
....

Date: .... / .... / ....

"The more grateful I am, the more beauty I see."
—Mary Davis

Today, I am grateful for...

1. ....
2. ....
3. ....

Goal for today...

....

Long-term goal I want to remember....

....

Daily affirmations—I am...

1. ....
2. ....

Time for prayer or reflection...

....
....
....
....
....

One win I had today was...

....
....

How could I have made today even better?

....
....

Date: .... / .... / ....

 Oh give thanks to the Lord, for he is good: for his steadfast love endures forever!
Psalm 118:1 (ESV)

Today, I am grateful for...

1. ....
2. ....
3. ....

Goal for today...

....

Long-term goal I want to remember....

....

Daily affirmations—I am...

1. ....
2. ....

Time for prayer or reflection...

....
....
....
....
....

One win I had today was...

....
....

How could I have made today even better?

....
....

Date: _____ / _____ / _____

 Challenge: *Take an evening walk without your phone.*

Today, I am grateful for...

1. ....
2. ....
3. ....

Goal for today...

....

Long-term goal I want to remember....

....

Daily affirmations—I am...

1. ....
2. ....

Time for prayer or reflection...

....
....
....
....
....

One win I had today was...

....
....

How could I have made today even better?

....
....

Date: _____ / _____ / _____

 "Character cannot be developed in ease and quiet. Only through experience of trial and suffering can the soul be strengthened, ambition inspired, and success achieved." –Hellen Keller

Today, I am grateful for...

1. ....
2. ....
3. ....

Goal for today...

....

Long-term goal I want to remember....

....

Daily affirmations—I am...

1. ....
2. ....

Time for prayer or reflection...

....
....
....
....

One win I had today was...

....
....

How could I have made today even better?

....
....

Date: .... / .... / ....

"Things must be felt with the heart."
—Helen Keller

Today, I am grateful for...

1. ....
2. ....
3. ....

Goal for today...

....

Long-term goal I want to remember....

....

Daily affirmations—I am...

1. ....
2. ....

Time for prayer or reflection...

....
....
....
....
....

One win I had today was...

....
....

How could I have made today even better?

....
....

Date: .... / .... / ....

 "Gratitude will shift you to a higher frequency, and you will attract much better things."
–Rhonda Byrne

Today, I am grateful for...

1. ....
2. ....
3. ....

Goal for today...

....

Long-term goal I want to remember....

....

Daily affirmations—I am...

1. ....
2. ....

Time for prayer or reflection...

....
....
....
....
....

One win I had today was...

....
....

How could I have made today even better?

....
....

Date: .... / .... / ....

 "Being thankful for something instantly grants that thing a depth it would not have had were I not thankful for it. And while I can certainly live without having had that kind of depth, in turn I will have died without ever having had any kind of life." —Craig D. Lounsbrough

Today, I am grateful for...

1. ....
2. ....
3. ....

Goal for today...

....

Long-term goal I want to remember....

....

Daily affirmations—I am...

1. ....
2. ....

Time for prayer or reflection...

....
....
....
....
....

One win I had today was...

....
....

How could I have made today even better?

....
....

Date: _____ / _____ / _____

 "We can complain because rose bushes have thorns or rejoice because thorns have roses."
—Alphonse Karr

Today, I am grateful for...

1. ....
2. ....
3. ....

Goal for today...

....

Long-term goal I want to remember....

....

Daily affirmations—I am...

1. ....
2. ....

Time for prayer or reflection...

....
....
....
....

One win I had today was...

....
....

How could I have made today even better?

....
....

Date: _____ / _____ / _____

"A sense of blessedness comes from a change of heart, not from more blessings."
—Mason Cooley

Today, I am grateful for...

1. ....
2. ....
3. ....

Goal for today...

....

Long-term goal I want to remember....

....

Daily affirmations—I am...

1. ....
2. ....

Time for prayer or reflection...

....
....
....
....
....

One win I had today was...

....
....

How could I have made today even better?

....
....

Date: ..../......../..........

 Challenge: *Call a friend or family member to tell them you care about them.*

Today, I am grateful for...

1. ....
2. ....
3. ....

Goal for today...

....

Long-term goal I want to remember....

....

Daily affirmations—I am...

1. ....
2. ....

Time for prayer or reflection...

....
....
....
....

One win I had today was...

....
....

How could I have made today even better?

....
....

Date: _____ / _____ / _____

 "In the middle of difficulty lies opportunity."
—Albert Einstein

Today, I am grateful for...

1. _____
2. _____
3. _____

Goal for today...

_____

Long-term goal I want to remember....

_____

Daily affirmations—I am...

1. _____
2. _____

Time for prayer or reflection...

_____
_____
_____
_____

One win I had today was...

_____
_____

How could I have made today even better?

_____
_____

Date: ..../.........../..................

Sing to the Lord with thanksgiving; make melody to our God on the lyre!
He covers the heavens with clouds; he prepares rain for the earth; he makes
grass grow on the hills. Psalm 147:7-8 (ESV)

Today, I am grateful for...

1. ....
2. ....
3. ....

Goal for today...

....

Long-term goal I want to remember....

....

Daily affirmations—I am...

1. ....
2. ....

Time for prayer or reflection...

....
....
....
....

One win I had today was...

....
....

How could I have made today even better?

....
....

Date: ..../........../..................

"In ordinary life, we hardly realize that we receive a great deal more than we give, and that it is only with gratitude that life becomes rich." —Dietrich Bonhoeffer

Today, I am grateful for...

1. ....
2. ....
3. ....

Goal for today...

....

Long-term goal I want to remember....

....

Daily affirmations—I am...

1. ....
2. ....

Time for prayer or reflection...

....
....
....
....
....

One win I had today was...

....
....

How could I have made today even better?

....
....

Date: _____ / _____ / _____

"We often take for granted the very things that most deserve our gratitude."
—Cynthia Ozick

Today, I am grateful for...

1. ....
2. ....
3. ....

Goal for today...

....

Long-term goal I want to remember....

....

Daily affirmations—I am...

1. ....
2. ....

Time for prayer or reflection...

....
....
....
....
....

One win I had today was...

....
....

How could I have made today even better?

....

Date: _____ / _____ / _____

"When you are grateful, fear disappears, and abundance appears."
—Tony Robbins

Today, I am grateful for...

1. ....
2. ....
3. ....

Goal for today...

....

Long-term goal I want to remember....

....

Daily affirmations—I am...

1. ....
2. ....

Time for prayer or reflection...

....
....
....
....
....

One win I had today was...

....
....

How could I have made today even better?

....
....

Date: .... / .... / ....

"For I know the plans I have for you," declares the Lord, "plans to prosper and not to harm you, plans to give you hope and a future." Jeremiah 29:11 (NIV)

Today, I am grateful for...

1. ....
2. ....
3. ....

Goal for today...

....

Long-term goal I want to remember....

....

Daily affirmations—I am...

1. ....
2. ....

Time for prayer or reflection...

....
....
....
....
....

One win I had today was...

....
....

How could I have made today even better?

....
....

Date: .... / .... / ....

"Wear gratitude like a cloak, and it will feed every corner of your life."
—Rumi

Today, I am grateful for...

1. ....
2. ....
3. ....

Goal for today...

....

Long-term goal I want to remember....

....

Daily affirmations—I am...

1. ....
2. ....

Time for prayer or reflection...

....
....
....
....
....

One win I had today was...

....
....

How could I have made today even better?

....
....

Date: .... / .... / ....

 Challenge: *Avoid sugary food and drinks today.*

Today, I am grateful for...

1. ....
2. ....
3. ....

Goal for today...

....

Long-term goal I want to remember....

....

Daily affirmations—I am...

1. ....
2. ....

Time for prayer or reflection...

....
....
....
....

One win I had today was...

....
....

How could I have made today even better?

....
....

Date: .... / .... / ....

"Nothing is more honorable than a grateful heart."
—Lucius Annaeus Seneca

Today, I am grateful for...

1. ....
2. ....
3. ....

Goal for today...

....

Long-term goal I want to remember....

....

Daily affirmations—I am...

1. ....
2. ....

Time for prayer or reflection...

....
....
....
....

One win I had today was...

....
....

How could I have made today even better?

....
....

Date: _____ / _____ / _____

"What separates privilege from entitlement is gratitude."
—Brené Brown

Today, I am grateful for...

1. ....
2. ....
3. ....

Goal for today...

....

Long-term goal I want to remember....

....

Daily affirmations—I am...

1. ....
2. ....

Time for prayer or reflection...

....
....
....
....

One win I had today was...

....
....

How could I have made today even better?

....
....

Date: _____ / _____ / _____

"What if we could actually get to the place where we thanked God for letting us face this battle because of the rich treasures we discovered on the battlefield?" —Lysa TerKeurst

Today, I am grateful for...

1. ....
2. ....
3. ....

Goal for today...

....

Long-term goal I want to remember....

....

Daily affirmations—I am...

1. ....
2. ....

Time for prayer or reflection...

....
....
....
....
....

One win I had today was...

....
....

How could I have made today even better?

....
....

Date: ..../........./...............

 "Gratitude is the healthiest of all human emotions. The more you express gratitude for what you have, the more likely you will have even more to express gratitude for."—Zig Ziglar

Today, I am grateful for...

1. ....
2. ....
3. ....

Goal for today...

....

Long-term goal I want to remember....

....

Daily affirmations—I am...

1. ....
2. ....

Time for prayer or reflection...

....
....
....
....

One win I had today was...

....
....

How could I have made today even better?

....
....

Date: _____ / _____ / _____

"Gratitude is when memory is stored in the heart and not in the mind."
—Lionel Hampton

Today, I am grateful for...

1. ....
2. ....
3. ....

Goal for today...

....

Long-term goal I want to remember....

....

Daily affirmations—I am...

1. ....
2. ....

Time for prayer or reflection...

....
....
....
....

One win I had today was...

....
....

How could I have made today even better?

....
....

"Be grateful for what you have and stop complaining—it bores everybody else, does you no good, and doesn't solve any problems." —Zig Ziglar

Today, I am grateful for...

1. ....
2. ....
3. ....

Goal for today...

....

Long-term goal I want to remember....

....

Daily affirmations—I am...

1. ....
2. ....

Time for prayer or reflection...

....
....
....
....

One win I had today was...

....
....

How could I have made today even better?

....
....

Date: _____ / _____ / _____

 Challenge: *Treat yourself! You have worked hard and deserve a special treat.*

Today, I am grateful for...

1. ....
2. ....
3. ....

Goal for today...

....

Long-term goal I want to remember....

....

Daily affirmations—I am...

1. ....
2. ....

Time for prayer or reflection...

....
....
....
....
....

One win I had today was...

....
....

How could I have made today even better?

....
....

Date: .... / .... / ....

Therefore let us be grateful for receiving a kingdom that cannot be shaken, and thus
let us offer to God acceptable worship, with reverence and awe, for our God is a consuming fire.
Hebrews 12:28-29 (ESV)

Today, I am grateful for...

1. ....
2. ....
3. ....

Goal for today...

....

Long-term goal I want to remember....

....

Daily affirmations—I am...

1. ....
2. ....

Time for prayer or reflection...

....
....
....
....
....

One win I had today was...

....
....

How could I have made today even better?

....
....

Date: _____ / _____ / _____

*"Gratitude unlocks the fullness of life. It turns what we have into enough, and more.
It turns denial into acceptance, chaos to order, confusion to clarity.
It can turn a meal into a feast, a house into a home, a stranger into a friend."—Melody Beattie*

Today, I am grateful for...

1. ....
2. ....
3. ....

Goal for today...

....

Long-term goal I want to remember....

....

Daily affirmations—I am...

1. ....
2. ....

Time for prayer or reflection...

....
....
....
....
....

One win I had today was...

....
....

How could I have made today even better?

....
....

Date: .... / .... / ....

 "It doesn't matter how slow you go as long as you don't stop." —Confucius

Today, I am grateful for...

1. ....
2. ....
3. ....

Goal for today...

....

Long-term goal I want to remember....

....

Daily affirmations—I am...

1. ....
2. ....

Time for prayer or reflection...

....
....
....
....

One win I had today was...

....
....

How could I have made today even better?

....
....

Date: .... / .... / ....

"There are only two ways to live your life. One is as though nothing is a miracle.
The other is as though everything is a miracle."—Albert Einstein

Today, I am grateful for...

1. ....
2. ....
3. ....

Goal for today...

....

Long-term goal I want to remember....

....

Daily affirmations—I am...

1. ....
2. ....

Time for prayer or reflection...

....
....
....
....
....

One win I had today was...

....
....

How could I have made today even better?

....
....

Date: .... / .... / ....

 Give thanks in all circumstances; for this is the will of God in Christ Jesus for you.
1 Thessalonians 5:18 (ESV)

Today, I am grateful for...

1. ....
2. ....
3. ....

Goal for today...

....

Long-term goal I want to remember....

....

Daily affirmations—I am...

1. ....
2. ....

Time for prayer or reflection...

....
....
....
....
....

One win I had today was...

....
....

How could I have made today even better?

....
....

Date: .... / .... / ....

"When we focus on our gratitude, the tide of disappointment goes out, and the tide of love rushes in."
—Kristin Armstrong

Today, I am grateful for...

1. ....
2. ....
3. ....

Goal for today...

....

Long-term goal I want to remember....

....

Daily affirmations—I am...

1. ....
2. ....

Time for prayer or reflection...

....
....
....
....
....

One win I had today was...

....
....

How could I have made today even better?

....
....

Date: .... / .... / ....

Challenge: *Stretch for 5-10 minutes.*

Today, I am grateful for...

1. ....
2. ....
3. ....

Goal for today...

....

Long-term goal I want to remember....

....

Daily affirmations—I am...

1. ....
2. ....

Time for prayer or reflection...

....
....
....
....
....

One win I had today was...

....
....

How could I have made today even better?

....
....

Date: .... / .... / ....

"Believe you can and you're halfway there."
—Theodore Roosevelt

Today, I am grateful for...

1. ....
2. ....
3. ....

Goal for today...

....

Long-term goal I want to remember....

....

Daily affirmations—I am...

1. ....
2. ....

Time for prayer or reflection...

....
....
....
....
....

One win I had today was...

....
....

How could I have made today even better?

....
....

Date: .... / .... / ....

"Gratitude is one of the most medicinal emotions we can feel.
It elevates our moods and fills us with joy." —Sara Avant Stover

Today, I am grateful for...

1. ....
2. ....
3. ....

Goal for today...

....

Long-term goal I want to remember....

....

Daily affirmations—I am...

1. ....
2. ....

Time for prayer or reflection...

....
....
....
....

One win I had today was...

....
....

How could I have made today even better?

....
....

Date: .... / .... / ....

But he said to me, "My grace is sufficient for you, for my power is made perfect in weakness."
Therefore I will boast all the more gladly of my weaknesses, so that the power of Christ
may rest upon me. 2 Corinthians 12:9 (NIV)

Today, I am grateful for...

1. ....
2. ....
3. ....

Goal for today...

....

Long-term goal I want to remember....

....

Daily affirmations—I am...

1. ....
2. ....

Time for prayer or reflection...

....
....
....
....

One win I had today was...

....
....

How could I have made today even better?

....
....

Date: .... / .... / ....

"If a fellow isn't thankful for what he's got, he isn't likely to be thankful for what he's going to get." —Frank A. Clark

Today, I am grateful for...

1. ....
2. ....
3. ....

Goal for today...

....

Long-term goal I want to remember....

....

Daily affirmations—I am...

1. ....
2. ....

Time for prayer or reflection...

....
....
....
....
....

One win I had today was...

....
....

How could I have made today even better?

....
....

Date: _____ / _____ / _____

*"Nothing new can come into your life unless you are grateful
for what you already have."* —Michael Bernhard

Today, I am grateful for...

1. ....
2. ....
3. ....

Goal for today...

....

Long-term goal I want to remember....

....

Daily affirmations—I am...

1. ....
2. ....

Time for prayer or reflection...

....
....
....
....
....

One win I had today was...

....
....

How could I have made today even better?

....
....

Date: _____ / _____ / _____

"Gratitude can transform common days into thanksgiving, turn routine jobs into joy, and change ordinary opportunities into blessings." —William Arthur Ward

Today, I am grateful for...

1. ....
2. ....
3. ....

Goal for today...

....

Long-term goal I want to remember....

....

Daily affirmations—I am...

1. ....
2. ....

Time for prayer or reflection...

....
....
....
....

One win I had today was...

....
....

How could I have made today even better?

....
....

Date: _____ / _____ / _____

Challenge: *Take a moment before every meal today to be thankful for it.*
That food is helping to make your life possible.

Today, I am grateful for...

1. ....
2. ....
3. ....

Goal for today...

....

Long-term goal I want to remember....

....

Daily affirmations—I am...

1. ....
2. ....

Time for prayer or reflection...

....
....
....
....
....

One win I had today was...

....
....

How could I have made today even better?

....
....

Date: .... / .... / ....

 Oh give thanks to the Lord; call upon his name; make known his deeds among the peoples!
1 Chronicles 16:8 (ESV)

Today, I am grateful for...

1. ....
2. ....
3. ....

Goal for today...

....

Long-term goal I want to remember....

....

Daily affirmations—I am...

1. ....
2. ....

Time for prayer or reflection...

....
....
....
....
....

One win I had today was...

....
....

How could I have made today even better?

....
....

Date: .... / .... / ....

Today, I am grateful for...

1. ....
2. ....
3. ....

Goal for today...

....

Long-term goal I want to remember....

....

Daily affirmations—I am...

1. ....
2. ....

Time for prayer or reflection...

....
....
....
....
....

One win I had today was...

....
....

How could I have made today even better?

....
....

Date: .... / .... / ....

 "The real gift of gratitude is that the more grateful you are, the more present you become."
—Robert Holden

Today, I am grateful for...

1. ....
2. ....
3. ....

Goal for today...

....

Long-term goal I want to remember....

....

Daily affirmations—I am...

1. ....
2. ....

Time for prayer or reflection...

....
....
....
....
....

One win I had today was...

....
....

How could I have made today even better?

....
....

Date: ..../.........../....................

"I will love the light for it shows me the way, yet I will endure the darkness
because it shows me the stars." —Og Mandino

Today, I am grateful for...

1. ....
2. ....
3. ....

Goal for today...

....

Long-term goal I want to remember....

....

Daily affirmations—I am...

1. ....
2. ....

Time for prayer or reflection...

....
....
....
....
....

One win I had today was...

....
....

How could I have made today even better?

....
....

Date: .... / .... / ....

Oh give thanks to the Lord, for he is good; for his steadfast love endures forever!
1 Chronicles 16:34 (ESV)

Today, I am grateful for...

1. ....
2. ....
3. ....

Goal for today...

....

Long-term goal I want to remember....

....

Daily affirmations—I am...

1. ....
2. ....

Time for prayer or reflection...

....
....
....
....

One win I had today was...

....
....

How could I have made today even better?

....
....

Date: .... / .... / ....

"Develop an attitude of gratitude, and give thanks for everything that happens to you, knowing that every step forward is a step toward achieving something bigger and better than your current situation." —Brian Tracy

Today, I am grateful for...

1. ....
2. ....
3. ....

Goal for today...

....

Long-term goal I want to remember....

....

Daily affirmations—I am...

1. ....
2. ....

Time for prayer or reflection...

....
....
....
....

One win I had today was...

....
....

How could I have made today even better?

....
....

Date: _____ / _____ / _____

 Challenge: *Don't get on any social media accounts today.*

Today, I am grateful for...

1. ....
2. ....
3. ....

Goal for today...

....

Long-term goal I want to remember....

....

Daily affirmations—I am...

1. ....
2. ....

Time for prayer or reflection...

....
....
....
....
....

One win I had today was...

....
....

How could I have made today even better?

....
....

Date: .... / .... / ....

"Embrace uncertainty. Some of the most beautiful chapters in our lives won't have a title until much later." —Bob Goff

Today, I am grateful for...

1. ....
2. ....
3. ....

Goal for today...

....

Long-term goal I want to remember....

....

Daily affirmations—I am...

1. ....
2. ....

Time for prayer or reflection...

....
....
....
....
....

One win I had today was...

....
....

How could I have made today even better?

....
....

Date: _____ / _____ / _____

"Parents who want to raise grateful kids need to start by living grateful lives."
—Kristen Welch

Today, I am grateful for...

1. ....
2. ....
3. ....

Goal for today...

....

Long-term goal I want to remember....

....

Daily affirmations—I am...

1. ....
2. ....

Time for prayer or reflection...

....
....
....
....

One win I had today was...

....
....

How could I have made today even better?

....
....

Date: .... / .... / ....

 I will give to the Lord the thanks due to his righteousness, and I will sing praise to the name of the Lord, the Most High. Psalm 7:17 (ESV)

Today, I am grateful for...

1. ....
2. ....
3. ....

Goal for today...

....

Long-term goal I want to remember....

....

Daily affirmations—I am...

1. ....
2. ....

Time for prayer or reflection...

....
....
....
....
....

One win I had today was...

....
....

How could I have made today even better?

....
....

Date: _____ / _____ / _____

*"He is a wise man who does not grieve for the things which he has not,
but rejoices for those which he has." —Epictetus*

Today, I am grateful for...

1. ....
2. ....
3. ....

Goal for today...

....

Long-term goal I want to remember....

....

Daily affirmations—I am...

1. ....
2. ....

Time for prayer or reflection...

....
....
....
....

One win I had today was...

....
....

How could I have made today even better?

....
....

Date: _____ / _____ / _____

"Let us be grateful to the people who make us happy; they are the charming gardeners who make our souls blossom." —Marcel Proust

Today, I am grateful for...

1. ....
2. ....
3. ....

Goal for today...

....

Long-term goal I want to remember....

....

Daily affirmations—I am...

1. ....
2. ....

Time for prayer or reflection...

....
....
....
....
....

One win I had today was...

....
....

How could I have made today even better?

....
....

Date: .... / .... / ....

"Do not spoil what you have by desiring what you have not; remember that
what you now have was once among the things you only hoped for." —Epicurus

Today, I am grateful for...

1. ....
2. ....
3. ....

Goal for today...

....

Long-term goal I want to remember....

....

Daily affirmations—I am...

1. ....
2. ....

Time for prayer or reflection...

....
....
....
....
....

One win I had today was...

....
....

How could I have made today even better?

....
....

Date: .... / .... / ....

 Challenge: *Make a list of all the good qualities you have (5-10 things).*

Today, I am grateful for...

1. ....
2. ....
3. ....

Goal for today...

....

Long-term goal I want to remember....

....

Daily affirmations—I am...

1. ....
2. ....

Time for prayer or reflection...

....
....
....
....
....

One win I had today was...

....
....

How could I have made today even better?

....
....

Date: .... / .... / ....

 I will give thanks to the Lord with my whole heart; I will recount all of your wonderful deeds.
Psalm 9:1 (ESV)

Today, I am grateful for...

1. ....
2. ....
3. ....

Goal for today...

....

Long-term goal I want to remember....

....

Daily affirmations—I am...

1. ....
2. ....

Time for prayer or reflection...

....
....
....
....
....

One win I had today was...

....
....

How could I have made today even better?

....
....

Date: .... / .... / ....

"Go confidently in the direction of your dreams. Live the life you have imagined."
—Henry Thoreau

Today, I am grateful for...

1. ....
2. ....
3. ....

Goal for today...

....

Long-term goal I want to remember....

....

Daily affirmations—I am...

1. ....
2. ....

Time for prayer or reflection...

....
....
....
....
....

One win I had today was...

....
....

How could I have made today even better?

....
....

Date: .... / .... / ....

"Cultivate the habit of being grateful for every good thing that comes to you, and to give thanks continuously. And because all things have contributed to your advancement, you should include all things in your gratitude." —Ralph Waldo Emerson

Today, I am grateful for...

1. ....
2. ....
3. ....

Goal for today...

....

Long-term goal I want to remember....

....

Daily affirmations—I am...

1. ....
2. ....

Time for prayer or reflection...

....
....
....
....
....

One win I had today was...

....
....

How could I have made today even better?

....
....

Date: .... / .... / ....

"Anything's possible if you've got the nerve."
—J.K. Rowling

Today, I am grateful for...

1. ....
2. ....
3. ....

Goal for today...

....

Long-term goal I want to remember....

....

Daily affirmations—I am...

1. ....
2. ....

Time for prayer or reflection...

....
....
....
....

One win I had today was...

....
....

How could I have made today even better?

....
....

Date: .... / .... / ....

The Lord is my strength and my shield; in him my heart trusts, and I am helped;
my heart exults, and with my song I give thanks to him. Psalm 28:7 (ESV)

Today, I am grateful for...

1. ....
2. ....
3. ....

Goal for today...

....

Long-term goal I want to remember....

....

Daily affirmations—I am...

1. ....
2. ....

Time for prayer or reflection...

....
....
....
....

One win I had today was...

....
....

How could I have made today even better?

....
....

Date: _____ / _____ / _____

 "I would maintain that thanks are the highest form of thought, and that gratitude is happiness doubled by wonder." —Gilbert K. Chesterton

Today, I am grateful for...

1. ....
2. ....
3. ....

Goal for today...

....

Long-term goal I want to remember....

....

Daily affirmations—I am...

1. ....
2. ....

Time for prayer or reflection...

....
....
....
....
....

One win I had today was...

....
....

How could I have made today even better?

....
....

Date: .... / .... / ....

 Challenge: *Drink 64 ounces of water.*

Today, I am grateful for...

1. ....
2. ....
3. ....

Goal for today...

....

Long-term goal I want to remember....

....

Daily affirmations—I am...

1. ....
2. ....

Time for prayer or reflection...

....
....
....
....
....

One win I had today was...

....
....

How could I have made today even better?

....
....

Date: .... / .... / ....

"O Lord that lends me life, lend me a heart replete with thankfulness."
—William Shakespeare

Today, I am grateful for...

1. ....
2. ....
3. ....

Goal for today...

....

Long-term goal I want to remember....

....

Daily affirmations—I am...

1. ....
2. ....

Time for prayer or reflection...

....
....
....
....
....

One win I had today was...

....
....

How could I have made today even better?

....
....

Date: .... / .... / ....

"Appreciation can make a day, even change a life. Your willingness to put it into words is all that is necessary." —Margaret Cousins

Today, I am grateful for...

1. ....
2. ....
3. ....

Goal for today...

....

Long-term goal I want to remember....

....

Daily affirmations—I am...

1. ....
2. ....

Time for prayer or reflection...

....
....
....
....
....

One win I had today was...

....
....

How could I have made today even better?

....
....

Date: _____ / _____ / _____

I give thanks to my God always for you because of the grace of God that
was given you in Christ Jesus. 1 Corinthians 1:4 (ESV)

Today, I am grateful for...

1. ....
2. ....
3. ....

Goal for today...

....

Long-term goal I want to remember....

....

Daily affirmations—I am...

1. ....
2. ....

Time for prayer or reflection...

....
....
....
....
....

One win I had today was...

....
....

How could I have made today even better?

....
....

Date: .... / .... / ....

"Learn to be thankful for what you already have, while you pursue all that you want."
—Jim Rohn

Today, I am grateful for...

1. ....
2. ....
3. ....

Goal for today...

....

Long-term goal I want to remember....

....

Daily affirmations—I am...

1. ....
2. ....

Time for prayer or reflection...

....
....
....
....

One win I had today was...

....
....

How could I have made today even better?

....
....

Date: / /

"The roots of all goodness lie in the soil of appreciation for goodness."
—Dalai Lama

Today, I am grateful for...

1. ....
2. ....
3. ....

Goal for today...

....

Long-term goal I want to remember....

....

Daily affirmations—I am...

1. ....
2. ....

Time for prayer or reflection...

....
....
....
....
....

One win I had today was...

....
....

How could I have made today even better?

....
....

Date: .... / .... / ....

"Feeling gratitude and not expressing it is like wrapping a present and not giving it."
—William Arthur Ward

Today, I am grateful for...

1. ....
2. ....
3. ....

Goal for today...

....

Long-term goal I want to remember....

....

Daily affirmations—I am...

1. ....
2. ....

Time for prayer or reflection...

....
....
....
....

One win I had today was...

....
....

How could I have made today even better?

....
....

Date: _____ / _____ / _____

 Challenge: *Do something kind for someone else (double a tip,
pay for someone's meal, offer your spot in line, etc.)*

Today, I am grateful for...

1. ....
2. ....
3. ....

Goal for today...

....

Long-term goal I want to remember....

....

Daily affirmations—I am...

1. ....
2. ....

Time for prayer or reflection...

....
....
....
....
....

One win I had today was...

....
....

How could I have made today even better?

....
....

Date: <u>   </u> / <u>   </u> / <u>   </u>

And when he had given thanks, he broke it, and said, "This is my body, which is for you.
Do this in remembrance of me." 1 Corinthians 11:24 (ESV)

Today, I am grateful for...

1. ....
2. ....
3. ....

Goal for today...

....

Long-term goal I want to remember....

....

Daily affirmations—I am...

1. ....
2. ....

Time for prayer or reflection...

....
....
....
....
....

One win I had today was...

....
....

How could I have made today even better?

....
....

Date: _____ / _____ / _____

"Never let the odds keep you from doing what you know in your heart you were meant to do." —H. Jackson Brown Jr.

Today, I am grateful for...

1. ....
2. ....
3. ....

Goal for today...

....

Long-term goal I want to remember....

....

Daily affirmations—I am...

1. ....
2. ....

Time for prayer or reflection...

....
....
....
....
....

One win I had today was...

....
....

How could I have made today even better?

....
....

Date: .... / .... / ....

 "This a wonderful day. I've never seen this one before."
—Maya Angelou

Today, I am grateful for...

1. ....
2. ....
3. ....

Goal for today...

....

Long-term goal I want to remember....

....

Daily affirmations—I am...

1. ....
2. ....

Time for prayer or reflection...

....
....
....
....
....

One win I had today was...

....
....

How could I have made today even better?

....
....

Date: _____ / _____ / _____

"It doesn't matter who you are, where you come from. The ability to triumph begins with you. Always."
—Oprah Winfrey

Today, I am grateful for...

1. ....
2. ....
3. ....

Goal for today...

....

Long-term goal I want to remember....

....

Daily affirmations—I am...

1. ....
2. ....

Time for prayer or reflection...

....
....
....
....
....

One win I had today was...

....
....

How could I have made today even better?

....
....

Date: ..../........../..................

 But thanks be to God, who gives us victory through our Lord Jesus Christ.
1 Corinthians 15:57 (ESV)

Today, I am grateful for...

1. ....
2. ....
3. ....

Goal for today...

....

Long-term goal I want to remember....

....

Daily affirmations—I am...

1. ....
2. ....

Time for prayer or reflection...

....
....
....
....

One win I had today was...

....
....

How could I have made today even better?

....
....

Date: _____ / _____ / _____

"The secret of health for both mind and body is not to mourn for the past, not to worry about the future, but to live the present moment wisely and earnestly." —Buddha

Today, I am grateful for...

1. ....
2. ....
3. ....

Goal for today...

....

Long-term goal I want to remember....

....

Daily affirmations—I am...

1. ....
2. ....

Time for prayer or reflection...

....

....

....

....

....

One win I had today was...

....

....

How could I have made today even better?

....

....

Date: _____ / _____ / _____

Challenge: *Treat yourself to a nap.*

Today, I am grateful for...

1. ....
2. ....
3. ....

Goal for today...

....

Long-term goal I want to remember....

....

Daily affirmations—I am...

1. ....
2. ....

Time for prayer or reflection...

....
....
....
....

One win I had today was...

....
....

How could I have made today even better?

....
....

Date: .... / .... / ....

"And you ask 'What if I fall?' Oh but my darling, what if you fly?"
—Erin Hanson

Today, I am grateful for...

1. ....
2. ....
3. ....

Goal for today...

....

Long-term goal I want to remember....

....

Daily affirmations—I am...

1. ....
2. ....

Time for prayer or reflection...

....
....
....
....
....

One win I had today was...

....
....

How could I have made today even better?

....
....

Date: _____ / _____ / _____

 "Most of us, swimming against the tides of trouble the world knows nothing about, need only a bit of praise or encouragement – and we will make the goal." —Jerome Fleishman

Today, I am grateful for...

1. ....
2. ....
3. ....

Goal for today...

....

Long-term goal I want to remember....

....

Daily affirmations—I am...

1. ....
2. ....

Time for prayer or reflection...

....
....
....
....
....

One win I had today was...

....
....

How could I have made today even better?

....
....

Date: _____ / _____ / _____

 But thanks be to God, who in Christ always leads us in triumphal procession, and through us spreads the fragrance of the knowledge of him everywhere. 2 Corinthians 2:14 (ESV)

Today, I am grateful for...

1. ....
2. ....
3. ....

Goal for today...

....

Long-term goal I want to remember....

....

Daily affirmations—I am...

1. ....
2. ....

Time for prayer or reflection...

....
....
....
....
....

One win I had today was...

....
....

How could I have made today even better?

....
....

Date: .... / .... / ....

"What the caterpillar calls the end of the world, the master calls a butterfly."
—*Richard Bach*

Today, I am grateful for...

1. ....
2. ....
3. ....

Goal for today...

....

Long-term goal I want to remember....

....

Daily affirmations—I am...

1. ....
2. ....

Time for prayer or reflection...

....
....
....
....
....

One win I had today was...

....
....

How could I have made today even better?

....
....

Date: _____ / _____ / _____

 "Life is 10 percent what happens to me and 90 percent how I react to it."
—Charles Swindoll

Today, I am grateful for...

1. ....
2. ....
3. ....

Goal for today...

....

Long-term goal I want to remember....

....

Daily affirmations—I am...

1. ....
2. ....

Time for prayer or reflection...

....
....
....
....

One win I had today was...

....
....

How could I have made today even better?

....
....

Date: _____ / _____ / _____

 "Never give up, for that is just the place and time that the tide will turn."
—Harriet Beecher Stowe

Today, I am grateful for...

1. ....
2. ....
3. ....

Goal for today...

....

Long-term goal I want to remember....

....

Daily affirmations—I am...

1. ....
2. ....

Time for prayer or reflection...

....
....
....
....
....

One win I had today was...

....
....

How could I have made today even better?

....
....

Date: _____ / _____ / _____

Today, I am grateful for...

1. ....
2. ....
3. ....

Goal for today...

....

Long-term goal I want to remember....

....

Daily affirmations—I am...

1. ....
2. ....

Time for prayer or reflection...

....
....
....
....

One win I had today was...

....
....

How could I have made today even better?

....
....

Date: .... / .... / ....

"Expressing thankfulness energizes, enhances, and empowers."
—Skip Prichard

Today, I am grateful for...

1. ....
2. ....
3. ....

Goal for today...

....

Long-term goal I want to remember....

....

Daily affirmations—I am...

1. ....
2. ....

Time for prayer or reflection...

....
....
....
....

One win I had today was...

....
....

How could I have made today even better?

....
....

Date: .... / .... / ....

*"No one who achieves success does so without acknowledging the help of others.
The wise and confident acknowledge this help with gratitude." —Alfred North Whitehead*

Today, I am grateful for...

1. ....
2. ....
3. ....

Goal for today...

....

Long-term goal I want to remember....

....

Daily affirmations—I am...

1. ....
2. ....

Time for prayer or reflection...

....
....
....
....
....

One win I had today was...

....
....

How could I have made today even better?

....
....

Date: .... / .... / ....

"Gratitude is riches. Complaint is poverty."
—Doris Day

Today, I am grateful for...

1. ....
2. ....
3. ....

Goal for today...

....

Long-term goal I want to remember....

....

Daily affirmations—I am...

1. ....
2. ....

Time for prayer or reflection...

....
....
....
....
....

One win I had today was...

....
....

How could I have made today even better?

....
....

Date: _____ / _____ / _____

"I may not be where I want to be but I'm thankful for not being where I used to be."
—Habeeb Akande

Today, I am grateful for...

1. ....
2. ....
3. ....

Goal for today...

....

Long-term goal I want to remember....

....

Daily affirmations—I am...

1. ....
2. ....

Time for prayer or reflection...

....
....
....
....
....

One win I had today was...

....
....

How could I have made today even better?

....
....

Date: .... / .... / ....

 For it is all for your sake, so that as grace extends to more and more people it may increase thanksgiving, to the glory of God. 2 Corinthians 4:15 (ESV)

Today, I am grateful for...

1. ....
2. ....
3. ....

Goal for today...

....

Long-term goal I want to remember....

....

Daily affirmations—I am...

1. ....
2. ....

Time for prayer or reflection...

....
....
....
....
....

One win I had today was...

....
....

How could I have made today even better?

....
....

Date: _____ / _____ / _____

"Gratitude is the most exquisite form of courtesy."
—Jacques Maritain

Today, I am grateful for...

1. ....
2. ....
3. ....

Goal for today...

....

Long-term goal I want to remember....

....

Daily affirmations—I am...

1. ....
2. ....

Time for prayer or reflection...

....
....
....
....
....

One win I had today was...

....
....

How could I have made today even better?

....
....

Date: .... / .... / ....

 Challenge: *Write a kind review for a business where you had a positive experience.*

Today, I am grateful for...

1. ....
2. ....
3. ....

Goal for today...

....

Long-term goal I want to remember....

....

Daily affirmations—I am...

1. ....
2. ....

Time for prayer or reflection...

....
....
....
....
....

One win I had today was...

....
....

How could I have made today even better?

....
....

Date: .... / .... / ....

"No matter what you might be going through right now, God has blessed you far more than you probably imagine—not just with material goods, but with family, with freedom and with the ability to enjoy His gifts." —Billy Graham

Today, I am grateful for...

1. ....
2. ....
3. ....

Goal for today...

....

Long-term goal I want to remember....

....

Daily affirmations—I am...

1. ....
2. ....

Time for prayer or reflection...

....
....
....
....

One win I had today was...

....
....

How could I have made today even better?

....
....

Date: _____ / _____ / _____

 "Thank you' is the best prayer that anyone could say. I say that one a lot. Thank you expresses extreme gratitude, humility, understanding." —Alice Walker

Today, I am grateful for...

1. ....
2. ....
3. ....

Goal for today...

....

Long-term goal I want to remember....

....

Daily affirmations—I am...

1. ....
2. ....

Time for prayer or reflection...

....
....
....
....
....

One win I had today was...

....
....

How could I have made today even better?

....
....

Date: ..../ ..../ ....

Let there be no filthiness nor foolish talk nor crude joking, which are out of place, but
instead let there be thanksgiving. Ephesians 5:4 (ESV)

Today, I am grateful for...

1. ....
2. ....
3. ....

Goal for today...

....

Long-term goal I want to remember....

....

Daily affirmations—I am...

1. ....
2. ....

Time for prayer or reflection...

....
....
....
....
....

One win I had today was...

....
....

How could I have made today even better?

....
....

Date: .... / .... / ....

"Gratitude is the fairest blossom which springs from the soul."
—*Henry Ward Beecher*

Today, I am grateful for...

1. ....
2. ....
3. ....

Goal for today...

....

Long-term goal I want to remember....

....

Daily affirmations—I am...

1. ....
2. ....

Time for prayer or reflection...

....
....
....
....

One win I had today was...

....
....

How could I have made today even better?

....
....

Date: .... / .... / ....

 "Gratitude is a powerful catalyst for happiness. It's the spark that lights a fire of joy in your soul."
—Amy Collette

Today, I am grateful for...

1. ....
2. ....
3. ....

Goal for today...

....

Long-term goal I want to remember....

....

Daily affirmations—I am...

1. ....
2. ....

Time for prayer or reflection...

....
....
....
....

One win I had today was...

....
....

How could I have made today even better?

....
....

Date: .... / .... / ....

 "You cannot do a kindness too soon because you never know how soon it will be too late."
—Ralph Waldo Emerson

Today, I am grateful for...

1. ....
2. ....
3. ....

Goal for today...

....

Long-term goal I want to remember....

....

Daily affirmations—I am...

1. ....
2. ....

Time for prayer or reflection...

....
....
....
....

One win I had today was...

....
....

How could I have made today even better?

....
....

Date: _____ / _____ / _____

 Challenge: *What exercise are you thankful that you can do? Do it!*

Today, I am grateful for...

1. ....
2. ....
3. ....

Goal for today...

....

Long-term goal I want to remember....

....

Daily affirmations—I am...

1. ....
2. ....

Time for prayer or reflection...

....
....
....
....
....

One win I had today was...

....
....

How could I have made today even better?

....
....

Date: ..../ ..../ ....

 "Happiness is the condition of who we are and how we think and what we believe and how we live."
—Auliq Ice

Today, I am grateful for...

1. ....
2. ....
3. ....

Goal for today...

....

Long-term goal I want to remember....

....

Daily affirmations—I am...

1. ....
2. ....

Time for prayer or reflection...

....
....
....
....

One win I had today was...

....
....

How could I have made today even better?

....
....

Date: .... / .... / ....

 "Gratitude helps you to grow and expand; gratitude brings joy and laughter into your life and into the lives of all those around you." —Eileen Caddy

Today, I am grateful for...

1. ....
2. ....
3. ....

Goal for today...

....

Long-term goal I want to remember....

....

Daily affirmations—I am...

1. ....
2. ....

Time for prayer or reflection...

....
....
....
....
....

One win I had today was...

....
....

How could I have made today even better?

....
....

Date: _____ / _____ / _____

 "You may encounter many defeats, but you must not be defeated. In fact, it may be necessary to encounter the defeats, so you can know who you are, what you can rise from, how you can still come out of it." —Maya Angelou

Today, I am grateful for...

1. ....
2. ....
3. ....

Goal for today...

....

Long-term goal I want to remember....

....

Daily affirmations—I am...

1. ....
2. ....

Time for prayer or reflection...

....
....
....
....

One win I had today was...

....
....

How could I have made today even better?

....
....

Date: _____ / _____ / _____

 "Gratitude is not only the greatest of virtues, but the parent of all others."
—Marcus Tullius Cicero

Today, I am grateful for...

1. ....
2. ....
3. ....

Goal for today...

....

Long-term goal I want to remember....

....

Daily affirmations—I am...

1. ....
2. ....

Time for prayer or reflection...

....
....
....
....

One win I had today was...

....
....

How could I have made today even better?

....
....

Date: .... / .... / ....

 Do not be anxious about anything, but in everything by prayer and supplication with thanksgiving let your requests be made known to God. Philippians 4:6 (ESV)

Today, I am grateful for...

1. ....
2. ....
3. ....

Goal for today...

....

Long-term goal I want to remember....

....

Daily affirmations—I am...

1. ....
2. ....

Time for prayer or reflection...

....
....
....
....

One win I had today was...

....
....

How could I have made today even better?

....
....

Date: _____ / _____ / _____

 "Sometimes our light goes out but is blown into flame by another human being.
Each of us owes deepest thanks to those who have rekindled this light." —Albert Schweitzer

Today, I am grateful for...

1. ....
2. ....
3. ....

Goal for today...

....

Long-term goal I want to remember....

....

Daily affirmations—I am...

1. ....
2. ....

Time for prayer or reflection...

....
....
....
....

One win I had today was...

....
....

How could I have made today even better?

....
....

Date: .... / .... / ....

 Challenge: *Listen to a song that makes you smile.*

Today, I am grateful for...

1. ....
2. ....
3. ....

Goal for today...

....

Long-term goal I want to remember....

....

Daily affirmations—I am...

1. ....
2. ....

Time for prayer or reflection...

....
....
....
....
....

One win I had today was...

....
....

How could I have made today even better?

....
....

Date: .... / .... / ....

"Gratitude changes the pangs of memory into a tranquil joy."
—Dietrich Bonhoeffer

Today, I am grateful for...

1. ....
2. ....
3. ....

Goal for today...

....

Long-term goal I want to remember....

....

Daily affirmations—I am...

1. ....
2. ....

Time for prayer or reflection...

....
....
....
....
....

One win I had today was...

....
....

How could I have made today even better?

....
....

Date: _____ / _____ / _____

"I know that when I pray, something wonderful happens. Not just to the person or persons for whom I'm praying, but also something wonderful happens to me. I'm grateful that I'm heard." —Maya Angelou

Today, I am grateful for...

1. ....
2. ....
3. ....

Goal for today...

....

Long-term goal I want to remember....

....

Daily affirmations—I am...

1. ....
2. ....

Time for prayer or reflection...

....
....
....
....

One win I had today was...

....
....

How could I have made today even better?

....
....

Date: _____ / _____ / _____

 And whatever you do, in word or deed, do everything in the name of the Lord Jesus, giving thanks to God the Father through him. Colossians 3:17 (ESV)

Today, I am grateful for...

1. ....
2. ....
3. ....

Goal for today...

....

Long-term goal I want to remember....

....

Daily affirmations—I am...

1. ....
2. ....

Time for prayer or reflection...

....
....
....
....

One win I had today was...

....
....

How could I have made today even better?

....
....

Date: _____ / _____ / _____

"The unthankful heart...discovers no mercies; but let the thankful heart sweep through the day and, as the magnet finds the iron, so it will find, in every hour, some heavenly blessings!" —Henry Ward Beecher

Today, I am grateful for...

1. ....
2. ....
3. ....

Goal for today...

....

Long-term goal I want to remember....

....

Daily affirmations—I am...

1. ....
2. ....

Time for prayer or reflection...

....
....
....
....

One win I had today was...

....
....

How could I have made today even better?

....
....

Date: .... / .... / ....

"I'm grateful for always this moment, the now, no matter what form it takes."
—Eckhart Tolle

Today, I am grateful for...

1. ....
2. ....
3. ....

Goal for today...

....

Long-term goal I want to remember....

....

Daily affirmations—I am...

1. ....
2. ....

Time for prayer or reflection...

....
....
....
....
....

One win I had today was...

....
....

How could I have made today even better?

....
....

Date: ..../.........../...................

"There's no happier person than a truly thankful, content person."
—Joyce Meyer

Today, I am grateful for...

1. ....
2. ....
3. ....

Goal for today...

....

Long-term goal I want to remember....

....

Daily affirmations—I am...

1. ....
2. ....

Time for prayer or reflection...

....
....
....
....
....

One win I had today was...

....
....

How could I have made today even better?

....
....

Date: _____ / _____ / _____

 Challenge: *Turn a complaint into a blessing.*

Today, I am grateful for...

1. ....
2. ....
3. ....

Goal for today...

....

Long-term goal I want to remember....

....

Daily affirmations—I am...

1. ....
2. ....

Time for prayer or reflection...

....
....
....
....
....

One win I had today was...

....
....

How could I have made today even better?

....
....

Date: .... / .... / ....

For everything created by God is good, and nothing is to be rejected
if it is received with thanksgiving. 1 Timothy 4:4 (ESV)

Today, I am grateful for...

1. ....
2. ....
3. ....

Goal for today...

....

Long-term goal I want to remember....

....

Daily affirmations—I am...

1. ....
2. ....

Time for prayer or reflection...

....
....
....
....
....

One win I had today was...

....
....

How could I have made today even better?

....
....

Date: _____ / _____ / _____

"When it comes to life the critical thing is whether you take things for granted or take them with gratitude." —Gilbert K. Chesterton

Today, I am grateful for...

1. ....
2. ....
3. ....

Goal for today...

....

Long-term goal I want to remember....

....

Daily affirmations—I am...

1. ....
2. ....

Time for prayer or reflection...

....
....
....
....
....

One win I had today was...

....
....

How could I have made today even better?

....
....

Date: _____ / _____ / _____

"When you rise in the morning, give thanks for the light, for your life, for your strength. Give thanks for your food and for the joy of living. If you see no reason to give thanks, the fault lies in yourself." —Tecumseh

Today, I am grateful for...

1. ....
2. ....
3. ....

Goal for today...

....

Long-term goal I want to remember....

....

Daily affirmations—I am...

1. ....
2. ....

Time for prayer or reflection...

....
....
....
....
....

One win I had today was...

....
....

How could I have made today even better?

....
....

Date: .... / .... / ....

"Keep your eyes open to your mercies. The man who forgets to be thankful has fallen asleep in life." —Robert Louis Stevenson

Today, I am grateful for...

1. ....
2. ....
3. ....

Goal for today...

....

Long-term goal I want to remember....

....

Daily affirmations—I am...

1. ....
2. ....

Time for prayer or reflection...

....
....
....
....
....

One win I had today was...

....
....

How could I have made today even better?

....
....

Date: _____ / _____ / _____

 Saying, "Amen! Blessing and glory and wisdom and thanksgiving and honor and power and might be to our God forever and ever! Amen" Revelation 7:12 (ESV)

Today, I am grateful for...

1. ....
2. ....
3. ....

Goal for today...

....

Long-term goal I want to remember....

....

Daily affirmations—I am...

1. ....
2. ....

Time for prayer or reflection...

....
....
....
....

One win I had today was...

....
....

How could I have made today even better?

....
....

Date: .... / .... / ....

Today, I am grateful for...

1. ....
2. ....
3. ....

Goal for today...

....

Long-term goal I want to remember....

....

Daily affirmations—I am...

1. ....
2. ....

Time for prayer or reflection...

....
....
....
....
....

One win I had today was...

....
....

How could I have made today even better?

....
....

Date: .... / .... / ....

 Challenge: *Sit out in nature for 20 minutes without any technology.*

Today, I am grateful for...

1. ....
2. ....
3. ....

Goal for today...

....

Long-term goal I want to remember....

....

Daily affirmations—I am...

1. ....
2. ....

Time for prayer or reflection...

....
....
....
....

One win I had today was...

....
....

How could I have made today even better?

....
....

Date: .... / .... / ....

"Thankfulness is the beginning of gratitude. Gratitude is the completion of thankfulness. Thankfulness may consist merely of words. Gratitude is shown in acts." —Henri Frederic Amiel

Today, I am grateful for...

1. ....
2. ....
3. ....

Goal for today...

....

Long-term goal I want to remember....

....

Daily affirmations—I am...

1. ....
2. ....

Time for prayer or reflection...

....
....
....
....
....

One win I had today was...

....
....

How could I have made today even better?

....
....

Date: ..../ ..../ ....

 "I'm just thankful for everything, all the blessings in my life, trying to stay that way. I think that's the best way to start your day and finish your day. It keeps everything in perspective." —Tim Tebow

Today, I am grateful for...

1. ....
2. ....
3. ....

Goal for today...

....

Long-term goal I want to remember....

....

Daily affirmations—I am...

1. ....
2. ....

Time for prayer or reflection...

....
....
....
....
....

One win I had today was...

....
....

How could I have made today even better?

....
....

Date: _____ / _____ / _____

 Let them give thanks to the LORD for his unfailing love and his wonderful deeds for mankind, for he satisfies the thirsty and fills the hungry with good things. Psalm 107:8-9 (NIV)

Today, I am grateful for...

1. ....
2. ....
3. ....

Goal for today...

....

Long-term goal I want to remember....

....

Daily affirmations—I am...

1. ....
2. ....

Time for prayer or reflection...

....
....
....
....
....

One win I had today was...

....
....

How could I have made today even better?

....
....

"When you are grateful—when you can see what you have—you unlock blessings to flow in your life."
—*Suze Orman*

Today, I am grateful for...

1. ....
2. ....
3. ....

Goal for today...

....

Long-term goal I want to remember....

....

Daily affirmations—I am...

1. ....
2. ....

Time for prayer or reflection...

....
....
....
....
....

One win I had today was...

....
....

How could I have made today even better?

....
....

Date:

"Make it a habit to tell people thank you. To express your appreciation, sincerely and without the expectation of anything in return. Truly appreciate those around you, and you'll soon find many others around you. Truly appreciate life, and you'll find that you have more of it." —Ralph Marston

Today, I am grateful for...

1. ....
2. ....
3. ....

Goal for today...

....

Long-term goal I want to remember....

....

Daily affirmations—I am...

1. ....
2. ....

Time for prayer or reflection...

....
....
....
....
....

One win I had today was...

....
....

How could I have made today even better?

....
....

Date: .... / .... / ....

Today, I am grateful for...

1. ....
2. ....
3. ....

Goal for today...

....

Long-term goal I want to remember....

....

Daily affirmations—I am...

1. ....
2. ....

Time for prayer or reflection...

....
....
....
....
....

One win I had today was...

....
....

How could I have made today even better?

....
....

Date: .... / .... / ....

Today, I am grateful for...

1. ....
2. ....
3. ....

Goal for today...

....

Long-term goal I want to remember....

....

Daily affirmations—I am...

1. ....
2. ....

Time for prayer or reflection...

....
....
....
....

One win I had today was...

....
....

How could I have made today even better?

....
....

Date: .... / .... / ....

You will be enriched in every way so that you can be generous on every occasion,
and through us your generosity will result in thanksgiving to God.
2 Corinthians 9:11 (NIV)

Today, I am grateful for...

1. ....
2. ....
3. ....

Goal for today...

....

Long-term goal I want to remember....

....

Daily affirmations—I am...

1. ....
2. ....

Time for prayer or reflection...

....
....
....
....
....

One win I had today was...

....
....

How could I have made today even better?

....
....

Date: .... / .... / ....

"Whatever we are waiting for—peace of mind, contentment, grace, the inner awareness of simple abundance—it will surely come to us, but only when we are ready to receive it with an open and grateful heart." –Sarah Ban Breathnach

Today, I am grateful for...

1. ....
2. ....
3. ....

Goal for today...

....

Long-term goal I want to remember....

....

Daily affirmations—I am...

1. ....
2. ....

Time for prayer or reflection...

....
....
....
....
....

One win I had today was...

....
....

How could I have made today even better?

....
....

Date: _____ / _____ / _____

"I am thankful, of course, for the prize and thankful to God for each story, each idea, each word, each day." —Isaac Bashevis Singer

Today, I am grateful for...

1. ....
2. ....
3. ....

Goal for today...

....

Long-term goal I want to remember....

....

Daily affirmations—I am...

1. ....
2. ....

Time for prayer or reflection...

....
....
....
....
....

One win I had today was...

....
....

How could I have made today even better?

....
....

Date: _____ / _____ / _____

Today, I am grateful for...

1. ....
2. ....
3. ....

Goal for today...

....

Long-term goal I want to remember....

....

Daily affirmations—I am...

1. ....
2. ....

Time for prayer or reflection...

....
....
....
....
....

One win I had today was...

....
....

How could I have made today even better?

....
....

Date: .... / .... / ....

"Thanksgiving is recognition of a debt that cannot be paid. We express thanks,
whether or not we are able otherwise to reimburse the giver." —Billy Graham

Today, I am grateful for...

1. ....
2. ....
3. ....

Goal for today...

....

Long-term goal I want to remember....

....

Daily affirmations—I am...

1. ....
2. ....

Time for prayer or reflection...

....
....
....
....

One win I had today was...

....
....

How could I have made today even better?

....
....

Date: .... / .... / ....

"I believe that if you don't derive a deep sense of purpose from what you do, if you don't come radiantly alive several times a day, if you don't feel deeply grateful at the tremendous good fortune that has been bestowed on you, then you are wasting your life. And life is too short to waste." —Srikumar Rao

Today, I am grateful for...

1. ....
2. ....
3. ....

Goal for today...

....

Long-term goal I want to remember....

....

Daily affirmations—I am...

1. ....
2. ....

Time for prayer or reflection...

....
....
....
....
....

One win I had today was...

....
....

How could I have made today even better?

....
....

Date: .... / .... / ....

 Challenge: *Put your phone away when you get home from work.*

Today, I am grateful for...

1. ....
2. ....
3. ....

Goal for today...

....

Long-term goal I want to remember....

....

Daily affirmations—I am...

1. ....
2. ....

Time for prayer or reflection...

....
....
....
....
....

One win I had today was...

....
....

How could I have made today even better?

....
....

Date: .... / .... / ....

"We are in a wrong state of mind if we are not in a thankful state of mind."
—Charles Spurgeon

Today, I am grateful for...

1. ....
2. ....
3. ....

Goal for today...

....

Long-term goal I want to remember....

....

Daily affirmations—I am...

1. ....
2. ....

Time for prayer or reflection...

....
....
....
....
....

One win I had today was...

....
....

How could I have made today even better?

....
....

Date: _____ / _____ / _____

 "Talent is God-given; be humble. Fame is man-given; be thankful. Conceit is self-given; be careful."
—Harvey Mackay

Today, I am grateful for...

1. ....
2. ....
3. ....

Goal for today...

....

Long-term goal I want to remember....

....

Daily affirmations—I am...

1. ....
2. ....

Time for prayer or reflection...

....
....
....
....
....

One win I had today was...

....
....

How could I have made today even better?

....
....

Date: .... / .... / ....

Do not be anxious about anything, but in every situation, by prayer and petition,
with thanksgiving, present your requests to God. And the peace of God, which transcends
all understanding, will guard your hearts and your minds in Christ Jesus. Philippians 4:6-7 (NIV)

Today, I am grateful for...

1. ....
2. ....
3. ....

Goal for today...

....

Long-term goal I want to remember....

....

Daily affirmations—I am...

1. ....
2. ....

Time for prayer or reflection...

....
....
....
....
....

One win I had today was...

....
....

How could I have made today even better?

....
....

Date: _____ / _____ / _____

 "As with all commandments, gratitude is a description of a successful mode of living. The thankful heart opens our eyes to a multitude of blessings that continually surround us."
—James E. Faust

Today, I am grateful for...

1. ....
2. ....
3. ....

Goal for today...

....

Long-term goal I want to remember....

....

Daily affirmations—I am...

1. ....
2. ....

Time for prayer or reflection...

....
....
....
....

One win I had today was...

....
....

How could I have made today even better?

....
....

Date: .... / .... / ....

*"For what I have received may the Lord make me truly thankful.
And more truly for what I have not received." —Storm Jameson*

Today, I am grateful for...

1. ....
2. ....
3. ....

Goal for today...

....

Long-term goal I want to remember....

....

Daily affirmations—I am...

1. ....
2. ....

Time for prayer or reflection...

....
....
....
....
....

One win I had today was...

....
....

How could I have made today even better?

....
....

Date: _____ / _____ / _____

*"Often people ask how I manage to be happy despite having no arms and no legs.
The quick answer is that I have a choice. I can be angry about not having limbs,
or I can be thankful that I have a purpose. I chose gratitude." —Nick Vujicic*

Today, I am grateful for...

1. ....
2. ....
3. ....

Goal for today...

....

Long-term goal I want to remember....

....

Daily affirmations—I am...

1. ....
2. ....

Time for prayer or reflection...

....
....
....
....
....

One win I had today was...

....
....

How could I have made today even better?

....
....

Date: _____ / _____ / _____

Today, I am grateful for...

1. ....
2. ....
3. ....

Goal for today...

....

Long-term goal I want to remember....

....

Daily affirmations—I am...

1. ....
2. ....

Time for prayer or reflection...

....
....
....
....
....

One win I had today was...

....
....

How could I have made today even better?

....
....

Date: .... / .... / ....

 Fear not, for I am with you; be not dismayed, for I am your God; I will strengthen you, I will help you, I will uphold you with my righteous right hand. Isaiah 41:10 (NIV)

Today, I am grateful for...

1. ....
2. ....
3. ....

Goal for today...

....

Long-term goal I want to remember....

....

Daily affirmations—I am...

1. ....
2. ....

Time for prayer or reflection...

....
....
....
....
....

One win I had today was...

....
....

How could I have made today even better?

....
....

Date: .... / .... / ....

"I'm really thankful for every experience I've had, even the ones that were puzzling or disorienting, because they taught me so much." —Tavi Gevinson

Today, I am grateful for...

1. ....
2. ....
3. ....

Goal for today...

....

Long-term goal I want to remember....

....

Daily affirmations—I am...

1. ....
2. ....

Time for prayer or reflection...

....
....
....
....
....

One win I had today was...

....
....

How could I have made today even better?

....
....

Date: <u>   </u> / <u>   </u> / <u>   </u>

"We would worry less if we praised more. Thanksgiving is the enemy of discontent and dissatisfaction." —H.A. Ironside

Today, I am grateful for...

1. ....
2. ....
3. ....

Goal for today...

....

Long-term goal I want to remember....

....

Daily affirmations—I am...

1. ....
2. ....

Time for prayer or reflection...

....
....
....
....
....

One win I had today was...

....
....

How could I have made today even better?

....
....

Date: .... / .... / ....

"If you want to turn your life around, try thankfulness. It will change your life mightily."
—Gerald Good

Today, I am grateful for...

1. ....
2. ....
3. ....

Goal for today...

....

Long-term goal I want to remember....

....

Daily affirmations—I am...

1. ....
2. ....

Time for prayer or reflection...

....
....
....
....
....

One win I had today was...

....
....

How could I have made today even better?

....
....

Date: _____ / _____ / _____

Cast all your anxiety on Him because he cares for you.
1 Peter 5:7 (NIV)

Today, I am grateful for...

1. ....
2. ....
3. ....

Goal for today...

....

Long-term goal I want to remember....

....

Daily affirmations—I am...

1. ....
2. ....

Time for prayer or reflection...

....
....
....
....
....

One win I had today was...

....
....

How could I have made today even better?

....
....

Date: .... / .... / ....

"Sometimes we spend so much time and energy thinking about where we want to go that we don't notice where we happen to be." —Dan Gutman

Today, I am grateful for...

1. ....
2. ....
3. ....

Goal for today...

....

Long-term goal I want to remember....

....

Daily affirmations—I am...

1. ....
2. ....

Time for prayer or reflection...

....
....
....
....
....

One win I had today was...

....
....

How could I have made today even better?

....
....

Date: ..../ ..../ ....

Challenge: *Give someone a loving hug.*

Today, I am grateful for...

1. ....
2. ....
3. ....

Goal for today...

....

Long-term goal I want to remember....

....

Daily affirmations—I am...

1. ....
2. ....

Time for prayer or reflection...

....
....
....
....
....

One win I had today was...

....
....

How could I have made today even better?

....
....

Date: .... / .... / ....

"Whatever happens in your life, no matter how troubling things might seem, do not enter the neighborhood of despair. Even when all doors remain closed, God will open up a new path only for you. Be thankful!" —Elif Shafak

Today, I am grateful for...

1. ....
2. ....
3. ....

Goal for today...

....

Long-term goal I want to remember....

....

Daily affirmations—I am...

1. ....
2. ....

Time for prayer or reflection...

....
....
....
....
....

One win I had today was...

....
....

How could I have made today even better?

....
....

Date: _____ / _____ / _____

"Do not indulge in dreams of having what you have not, but reckon up the chief of the blessings you do possess, and then thankfully remember how you would crave for them if they were not yours." —Marcus Aurelius

Today, I am grateful for...

1. ....
2. ....
3. ....

Goal for today...

....

Long-term goal I want to remember....

....

Daily affirmations—I am...

1. ....
2. ....

Time for prayer or reflection...

....
....
....
....
....

One win I had today was...

....
....

How could I have made today even better?

....
....

Date: _____ / _____ / _____

Let the peace of Christ rule in your hearts, since as members of one body
you were called to peace. And be thankful.
Colossians 3:15 (NIV)

Today, I am grateful for...

1. ....
2. ....
3. ....

Goal for today...

....

Long-term goal I want to remember....

....

Daily affirmations—I am...

1. ....
2. ....

Time for prayer or reflection...

....
....
....
....
....

One win I had today was...

....
....

How could I have made today even better?

....
....

Date: .... / .... / ....

"Thankfulness creates gratitude which generates contentment that causes peace."
—Todd Stocker

Today, I am grateful for...

1. ....
2. ....
3. ....

Goal for today...

....

Long-term goal I want to remember....

....

Daily affirmations—I am...

1. ....
2. ....

Time for prayer or reflection...

....
....
....
....
....

One win I had today was...

....
....

How could I have made today even better?

....
....

Date: _____ / _____ / _____

 "Every once in a while God allows you to stub your toe as a kind reminder to be grateful for the miraculous body attached to it." —Richelle E. Goodrich

Today, I am grateful for...

1. ....
2. ....
3. ....

Goal for today...

....

Long-term goal I want to remember....

....

Daily affirmations—I am...

1. ....
2. ....

Time for prayer or reflection...

....
....
....
....
....

One win I had today was...

....
....

How could I have made today even better?

....
....

Date: .... / .... / ....

"Grumbling and gratitude are, for the child of God, in conflict. Be grateful and you won't grumble. Grumble and you won't be grateful." —Billy Graham

Today, I am grateful for...

1. ....
2. ....
3. ....

Goal for today...

....

Long-term goal I want to remember....

....

Daily affirmations—I am...

1. ....
2. ....

Time for prayer or reflection...

....
....
....
....

One win I had today was...

....
....

How could I have made today even better?

....
....

Date: .... / .... / ....

 This is the day that the LORD has made; let us rejoice and be glad in it.
Psalm 118:24 (NIV)

Today, I am grateful for...

1. ....
2. ....
3. ....

Goal for today...

....

Long-term goal I want to remember....

....

Daily affirmations—I am...

1. ....
2. ....

Time for prayer or reflection...

....
....
....
....
....

One win I had today was...

....
....

How could I have made today even better?

....
....

Date: ....../ ....../ ....

"We pray for the big things and forget to give thanks for the ordinary, small (and yet really not small) gifts." — Dietrich Bonhoeffer

Today, I am grateful for...

1. ....
2. ....
3. ....

Goal for today...

....

Long-term goal I want to remember....

....

Daily affirmations—I am...

1. ....
2. ....

Time for prayer or reflection...

....
....
....
....
....

One win I had today was...

....
....

How could I have made today even better?

....
....

Date: _____ / _____ / _____

 "The soul that gives thanks can find comfort in everything; the soul that complains can find comfort in nothing." —Hannah Whitall Smith

Today, I am grateful for...

1. ....
2. ....
3. ....

Goal for today...

....

Long-term goal I want to remember....

....

Daily affirmations—I am...

1. ....
2. ....

Time for prayer or reflection...

....
....
....
....
....

One win I had today was...

....
....

How could I have made today even better?

....
....

Date: .... / .... / ....

 "Gratitude is an overflow of the pleasure filling your soul."
—Raheel Farooq

Today, I am grateful for...

1. ....
2. ....
3. ....

Goal for today...

....

....

Long-term goal I want to remember....

....

....

Daily affirmations—I am...

1. ....
2. ....

Time for prayer or reflection...

....

....

....

....

....

One win I had today was...

....

....

How could I have made today even better?

....

....

Thank You

Thank you for welcoming me into your home to share my gratitude story with you. I hope your journey practicing gratitude helps you to become an even better you as you see all the blessings in your life.

If you enjoyed this book, it would mean so much to me if you wrote a review so other moms can read about your experience. Thanks!

Sincerely,

Autumn

PS-I would very much love to hear your gratitude story or offer an encouraging word, so please email me at autumn@bestmomideas.com.

Follow me at BestMomIdeas.com

 @bestmomideas   facebook.com/bestmomideas

Made in the USA
Las Vegas, NV
18 May 2021